THEN THERE '

B.P.SMYTHE.

B.P.SMYTHE.

B.P.Smythe studied engineering at Carshalton College and eventually became a member of the Institute of Quality Assurance.

For his published crime writing short stories and novels. B.P. Smythe was inducted into the Crime Writers Association for his achievements.

Sow And You Shall Reap - http://www.amazon.co.uk/dp/145677171X is his first self- published novel. Last year B.P. secured a three book deal of short stories from Bloodhound Books http://www.bloodhoundbooks.com/. His author bio is on their website.

From a Poison Pen is his first book of short stories http://www.amazon.co.uk/Poison-Pen-collection-macabre-stories-ebook/dp/B01BKWT4EE. His second book of short stories *From a Poison Pen VOL II* has just been released and is available on: https://www.amazon.co.uk/Poison-Pen-ii-B-P-Smythe-ebook/dp/B01LFM1032

This year 2017, B.P.Smythe is shortly to release two full length novels - *The Medal of Purity* and *The Expired* including two further books of short stories - *Short Tales with Long Memories VOL 1* and *VOL 2* and a novella - *The Holocaust Experience.*

B.P.SMYTHE Amazon author page: www.amazon.co.uk/-/e/B006MCGVNU

Books by B.P.Smythe For information on obtaining free complimentary PDF, Kindle or paperback copies, contact B.P.Smythe at barrysmythe@hotmail.com - Mob: 07814780856

B.P.Smythe short stories...barrysmythe@hotmail.com - Mob: 07814780856

THEN THERE WERE
NONE

Best Wishes Fiona

B. P.Smythe

B.P.SMYTHE.

Published by BM Smythe in 2018

ISBN: 978-1-911412-61-8

eBookS
Apple : 978-1-911412-62-5
Kindle: 978-1-911412-63-2

CONTENTS

THEN THERE WERE NONE.

B.P.SMYTHE.

An actress will stop at nothing including murder to get the right part for money and fame as she kills off the competition for a lucrative TV sitcom role.

film favourite *Kind Hearts and Coronets* with Dennis Price and Alec Guinness.

Later as the closing credits were going up, it suddenly occurred to her. Yes that was it. Get rid of the opposition. She had two months to do it in, but how? And get away with it?

She looked again at the list on her iPhone. In her haste to take the picture, she had included the small photo frame on the agent's desk. Having never been round the other side of his desk, she assumed it was a photo of his wife or family. Surprisingly it had no photo but there was some writing in copper plate style. Lydia leaned in closer. It was some sort of poem. She began to read.

Five pretty actresses at an audition on a call. However, one sits alone and plots the others tragic downfall.

First pretty actress learning how to ski, when suddenly she comes a cropper and gets injured fatally.

Second pretty actress driving as she sped. Then a life threatening car crash leaves her very dead.

Third pretty actress flying in the sky. When her aeroplane malfunctions, she knows she has to die.

Fourth pretty actress who's shooting skill is ace. Then a gun goes off she's using and blasts her in the face.

Fifth pretty actress, full of joy and glee. Has now the part she could wish for, but is she happy as can be?

Lydia thought for a while and read the poem again. She realised it could have been written for her. She'd certainly be happy if she had the part. The accident with the fourth pretty actress especially interested her. It was similar to the film she'd just watched. The shooting of the Duke of Chalfont while his foot was caught in a poachers trap. Yes that was it. Kill them off to the poem. They'll think it was the agent.

Lydia had met the four actresses at previous auditions. Previous auditions where each one of the bitches had been chosen for the main lead instead of her.

She remembered the plays. A Doll's House by Henrik Ibsen and how that tall, curvy figured, twenty-five year old, Dina Burlington, with her long platinum blonde hair and Nordic looks had mesmerised the theatre director. She'd been told by another cast member that the springs of his casting couch had probably worn out by the time of Dina's first dress rehearsal.

And then there was Steel Magnolias by Robert Harling. They gave that lead to Tracey Dunne. Twenty-six year old, medium height, slim figured Tracey. A redhead with a cute round face and a matching arse. Only the producer could have verified if she was a true redhead. Lydia had been told by a makeup artist, he'd spent more time in her dressing room than the clock on the wall.

Next came Lady Windermere's Fan by Oscar Wilde. Lydia had really wanted the Lady Windermere part. However, Susan Sinclair beat her to it. Not surprising. Twenty-eight year old Susan with her dark haired centre parting and flick-ups was a tall slim Sigourney Weaver look-a-like. Theatre impresario Victor Wiseman, who was the main financial backer, also picked her out from over

CHAPTER TWO

That weekend Lydia drove down in her five year old Fiesta to the *Shepherd and Lamb* pub in Newton Abbot. The plan was to book a room there overnight.

By Saturday mid-afternoon she'd swung into the gun club carpark at East Ogwell. The building hadn't changed much as far as could remember. At reception, while a woman was busy on the telephone, Lydia tried her pass.

She was ready with a sad story and to blub on call. Coming to collect her late father's beloved guns so they could be put in his coffin for the funeral next week and how they meant so much to him. Then to Lydia's relief the barrier swung open to let her through.

Out of the corner of her eye she saw her dated old pass photo come up on the reception computer screen.

With the rifle bag in full view that she'd bought on Amazon a few days earlier, Lydia made for the sign above a far door that stated **Gun Room.**

Immediately the faint smell of oil brought back memories. It hadn't changed much apart from some strip lighting and brown carpet tiles. Double checking the number on the pass and while three other elderly members fussed around their gun lockers, Lydia made her way along the narrow gangway until she came to her number on the steel door. She gave a furtive glance. No one gave her a second look. Lydia tried the key. It turned a little and then stuck. She cursed softly under her breath. Looking both ways she gave it a hard wriggle and then tried again. This time she heaved on the mother, her face screwing with exertion until - CLICK! The key turned all the way and the long narrow door swung open.

Lydia breathed in deep. There was her father's Ruger 10/22 rifle with a telescopic sight. With it were two boxes of .22 low noise hollow point shells. Also, wrapped in an oily smelly rag was a Ruger Mark III .22 semi-automatic pistol with a box of ammunition that he'd used on the range.

She carefully placed the weapons and ammunition in her gun bag and then locked the steel door. As she made her way to the reception exit barrier the woman behind the counter suddenly called her over. 'Excuse me. Don't forget to sign out and let me check your license and bag.'

Lydia flustered. 'Oh, of course, silly me.' She placed her gun bag on the counter and pulled her license and handed it across.

The receptionist peered in and checked the bag contents and then placed the gun license under a scanner and then returned it. Then she handed her a sign out weapons sheet to be completed.

Lydia knew the score. She had a story all ready.

Returning the sheet the receptionist smiled as she read her details. 'So you're doing the steel plate challenge at Budleigh Farm tomorrow.'

'Yes, I'm a bit rusty,' she said sheepishly, 'but I'm giving it a go.'

'Well best of luck to you and let's hope the weather stays fine.' With that the receptionist pressed the noisy buzzer under the counter which released the lock for the exit barrier.

Lydia smiled and said, 'Thanks,' as she passed through and made her way out to the carpark.

Inside her Fiesta, she gripped the steering wheel and breathed a sigh of relief. She couldn't believe it had been so easy.

By Sunday evening she was back home. She held the rifle and pistol in turn and took aim and then squeezed the trigger. They felt good in her hands. It had been some time. In fact she remembered, as her face darkened, the very last time.

*

Lydia was fostered out at two years old when the authorities had taken her away from her real single mother, a nineteen year old drug addict who later died of an overdose.

Her new parents had adopted her when they couldn't have any more children after their daughter Caroline was born.

Both girls grew up together. However it was Caroline who the parents doted on. She was the clever one who went to boarding school and then on to a good university.

While Lydia was groomed to be a farmer's wife, Caroline had met up with a lad at University with good social connections.

Jonathon Paul Barkworth came from a well healed family whose father was chairman of a hedge fund. Eventually at twenty-four years old, Caroline married her twenty-five year old fiancé.

For a while they lived on an estate in Berkshire in a wing of the family's mansion with a swimming pool, tennis court and horse riding stables. With their own privacy, everything seemed perfect at first. However the situation began to become tense for Caroline.

Jonathon's parents had thought he'd married beneath the family status. They were counting on a marriage to the likes of a chairman or a banker's daughter. Not a farmer's daughter. That's when Caroline's depression first took hold.

The following year the couple had a baby girl. Although Jonathon was over the moon, his parents still regarded Caroline and her farming family as gold diggers. Because she'd married their Jonathon she was accepted under sufferance.

Gradually it all became too much for Caroline. Her depression became more severe. She began to neglect her baby. Then chinks in the marriage began to appear. The little rows became big rows until Caroline decided to take the baby and return to her parent's farm in Devon.

Although Jonathon was heartbroken, his parents persuaded him it was for the best. The arrangements being he would come down to visit Caroline and the baby once a month.

Caroline's parents welcomed her and the baby with open arms. However, this wasn't the same for Lydia. The parents once again began to dote on their daughter and granddaughter. By now Lydia at twenty years old was helping full time on the farm. Then Lydia found drama. It was a new awakening. She mixed her time with farming and drama classes.

For Lydia she had to make the choice and London beckoned. She had been accepted at RADA.

When she told her parents she was leaving to pursue an acting career, they were angry and thought she was mad. A heated row followed. They called her ungrateful. Lydia's argument to them was, Caroline could help out now she'd returned.

They wouldn't listen and after that, relations became frosty.

Sometime later her parents had visited a solicitor in the town. She'd seen the exchange in letters on the doormat.

Lydia began to think about her parents will. She knew where it was kept - in a reproduction walnut bureau in the lounge. A key hung down the back on a piece of string. Her father kept his whiskey there for a quick snort. Away from the prying eyes of mother who was teetotal.

One Saturday morning as she watched her parents leave for the local market she saw her chance. With that lazy bitch still in bed and her baby not awake, she unlocked the bureau and quickly found the folder marked Marsland and Barber Solicitors and Co.

Lydia thumbed through the copy of the will dated three weeks ago. She read quickly through all the herewith's, aforsaid's, unto's, saidforth's and power of attorneys until she came to the nitty-gritty. Lydia leaned close and read. *And we leave seventy-five percent of our estate to our first born daughter Caroline, Lucy, Barkworth. And if on her death before our death. Then the share will be transferred to her daughter Amy, Christine, Barkworth. The remaining twenty-five percent of our estate we leave to our second daughter Lydia, Anne, Perkins.* Reading on it stated Lydia would only get full inheritance unless she survived them all.

She was seething. Lydia hated Caroline and her baby. And now she hated her parents.

She banged her fist on the bureau table. 'Shit!-Shit!-Shit!' She yelled. And then calmed down in case she was heard. 'Seventy-five percent to that lazy Bitch. No way,' she mumbled.

CHAPTER THREE

Lydia had it all planned. This last weekend of the month Jonathon as usual would be coming down to visit his wife and child.

That late Saturday afternoon the parents were watching television in the lounge. Caroline and Jonathan with the baby had discretely made themselves scarce and were upstairs in the bedroom. Her parents always hoped Caroline and Jonathan could work things out and get their marriage back on course again and thought it best they be left alone.

Lydia had made arrangements to go the cinema with a friend and was meeting her at 7:15p.m.

At 6:10 p.m., with the television blaring out the Generation Game, Lydia crept up the stairs with her father's 12 Bore over and under shotgun. His Ruger 10/22 rifle with the telescopic sight would have been better. It was lighter and easier to handle, but he kept that at the gun club for competitions. Still, at a time like this she couldn't be picky.

On the landing she saw their door was closed and it was quiet. Lydia moved forwards and gripped the brass handle. She slowly began to turn it.

The door inched open and they were in bed together with the baby asleep in its cot by the far wall. It was good their backs were to her. Lydia crept in. She had to get up close to make it look like suicide. She didn't have to worry about the noise of the blast. The next farmhouse along was three miles away.

The remains of a half smoked joint were in the ashtray. That was good. It would make them feel heady. Perhaps numb the senses.

Lydia checked the baby. It appeared to be sound asleep. With one eye on the cot, she tip-toed nearer. Lydia knew she was at the point of no return. As the barrel of the rifle came within an inch of Caroline's mouth she began to shake. She pulled away and took some deep silent breaths. Then she focused again, bringing the barrel down. Lydia steadied herself.

Just then the baby snuffled and fidgeted. Lydia froze and waited. After ten seconds all was quiet. She checked Jonathan, he was sound asleep.

Lydia swallowed hard and using the barrel, nudged Caroline's chin.

She instantly opened her eyes and as she began to scream, Lydia forced the barrel into her mouth. Lydia motioned for her to sit up. With the barrel in her mouth, Caroline gave out a muffled cry. Then Lydia squeezed the trigger.

The blast was deafening. The back of Caroline's head peppered the pillows with bone and blood, with some spattering Lydia's face and chest.

The baby was crying now and she had to be quick. As Jonathan half raised himself, Lydia took aim and shot him between the eyes. The blast sent him spiralling out of the bed.

He lay there on his back staring at the ceiling.

With the baby screaming its head off, Lydia reloaded and moved to the cot. She whispered to herself, 'God forgive me,' and closed her eyes as she pulled the trigger.

Now she had to be quick. Lydia could hear her parents calling. They must have heard the gunshots over the television. She reloaded again and as she moved out onto the landing her parents were coming up the stairs. She levelled the rifle. They stopped halfway up in amazement.

Lydia fired off two clear head shots. They were dead before they'd toppled back down to the bottom of the stairs.

Next, she had to arrange the scene to look as though Caroline had lost it with her depression and killed them all and shot herself through the mouth.

Returning to the bedroom, Lydia carefully wrapped Caroline's dead hands around the gun, leaving as many fingerprints as possible. Then she laid the shotgun on Caroline's blood spattered nightdress with the barrel pointing towards her face and the thumb of her right hand still resting on the trigger.

She took a step back. It look realistic enough and the gunshot residue on the trigger hand would be an added confirmation.

Satisfied, Lydia moved into the en suite bathroom and took a shower.

After a thorough clean-up of the tiles and tray, while double checking for traces of blood, Lydia emerged drying herself. After one last scan of the bedroom she made her way to her own room to get dressed.

Holding a bin liner containing her blood spattered clothes she carefully stepped over her parent's bodies to reach the front door. With a last minute look she closed it behind her and climbed into her Peugeot 1100.

*

By the time Lydia had arrived home from the cinema she had practised her hysteric 999 emergency call many times.

Making herself comfortable in the kitchen she tried it one more time and then dialled the police using her mobile. 'Emergency! – Emergency!' she shouted. 'Oh Jesus! they're all dead. Quick get someone to the house. They've all been murdered.' Gulp – Sob. 'There's blood everywhere,' she blabbed.

Within seconds the BT operator had transferred Lydia to the local Force Control Room. In-between calming her down they began to take details. Lydia explained she had run out of the house in case whoever did it was still around.

She told them she'd be waiting at the end of the farmhouse drive.

The killings had been news for weeks. In the meantime she stayed with a friend until the farm was sold. The big shock came at the reading of the will. Apparently her parents had taken out equity release on the farmhouse for a loan. Unbeknown to Lydia that's how they'd maintained their comfortable lifestyle. That meant after expenses and a costly funeral headstone that had been pre-ordered, she was left with only a third of what she'd hoped for.

CHAPTER FOUR

Lydia poured herself a glass of wine and sat back on the sofa. Although the incident happened fourteen years ago, it was the day that changed her life. Lydia knew something inside had snapped. She could never get close or love anything.

She'd been a number of times to a private physiatrist. Done the tests for word association as well as the Rorschach inkblot test. Been given Sodium Pentothal and Scopolomine, a truth serum under hypnosis. Then diagnosed. Been told in a bed side manner that she had no empathy or lack of remorse and was deceitful. And suffered from alcohol and drug abuse. She'd admitted she drank too much and did cocaine when she could afford it. She had addictive behaviour. That was true. Her iPhone gambling debts confirmed that. However, drama was a let out, her saviour. It was a release valve in her head. When she was acting she was in another world and nothing else mattered. And to be famous was the icing on the cake. And how she yearned to be famous and show all those shmucks who'd put her down over the years, this lady had made it to the top.

Lydia picked up the list and took a heavy swig of wine. She said with a twisted smile. 'You might have won the audition, girls, but I'll make sure you have a day out you'll never forget.'

*

Tracey Dunne was all excited. This morning she'd taken delivery of a letter with a bunch of Magnolias. The events card entitled her to a day out on an artificial ski slope at Borehamwood. All paid for by *PINK LETTER DAYS*. At the bottom it was signed Have a great day out. Will be in touch next week. X

Someone connected to Steel Magnolias, the play she appeared in, had briefly crossed her mind. There were one or two in the cast that could have sent the flowers and card. Then again it could be her best friend Millie? Ian her live in boyfriend was adamant they hadn't come from him. And secretly he was a bit worried they could have come from some bloke sniffing around his girlfriend.

After convincing her boyfriend he had nothing to worry about, Tracey set off and arrived at Borehamwood ski complex. The first thing she noticed was how steep the ski runs were and the variety of slopes. Tracey had been on nine skiing holidays so far. Mostly to Val Louron, Tignes and Chamonix. This and practicing at the Sandown Ski Complex in Esher had allowed her to progress from the nursery slopes for beginners to the red slopes for intermediate users. She had mastered a control of speed and could link snowplough turns, going parallel and finishing with an arc turn with the skis on edge.

With three others, two men and a woman who were also on an events day out, wearing a helmet, knee padded dry slope slacks and elbow padded tops with gloves, they were greeted by their ski instructor for the day. Kristian was a dishy twenty-six year old from France and spoke with a heavy accent.

Tracey liked it when she was being held by Kristian while he showed her some of the advanced skiing moves during the morning training. Then she followed behind Kristian in a single chair lift, up to the highest slope.

With the two men on the nursery slope, Lydia with the other woman and Kristian set off and came down the red dry slope twisting and turning and finished with an arc turn at the bottom.

'Jesus, that was fantastic. So invigorating,' she told Kristian. He flashed her a smile back showing a perfect set of white teeth.

Within five minutes the three of them were at the front of the queue and boarded their ski lift chairs to the top again.

Lydia had come into the centre earlier holding her ski bag with a rifle concealed inside. Wearing a one piece ski suit she had climbed and positioned herself up in the ski lift gantry structure of the adjacent slope.

Lydia was perfectly hidden between the interwoven mazes of pylons and had a good view of the ski lift chairs.

Using her father's Ruger 10/22 rifle with a telescopic sight, she had to make sure the low noise .22 hollow point shells would shatter the small diameter shaft of the cable clamping mechanism. She knew she had only one chance.

Taking aim, she waited for Tracey's chair to come into view. In the telescopic sight she lined up the small shaft in the cable clamping mechanism. Then Lydia squeezed the trigger. Suddenly there was a crack like a pistol shot and the chair lift sagged, as if hung by a thread. Tracey cried out. *'Christ, what was that?'* She was holding on, half in, half out of her tipped chair. She looked up and froze in fear. The chair was still moving, climbing higher.

Tracey heard another crack and the chair sagged further tipping her more. She started yelling, *'Help me for Christ sake. Stop the bloody thing.'*

People in the chair lift coming down looked on in horror as they passed.

Kristian who was ahead, turned and motioned for her to keep still. He pulled his mobile and began to phone the wheel house to let them know they had an emergency on the ski lift. Suddenly there was a further crack. Tracey screamed, *'Oh my God. Help me,'* as she was tipped out and left dangling with both hands clutching the safety rail.

She hung there for a few seconds and then came a final crack.

Tracey screamed again as she and the chair plunged over ninety feet to the ground below. As she hit the dry slope the chair smashed on top of her.

Looking through the telescopic sight, Lydia could see no movement. It would appear she was very dead. Within minutes a crowd had gathered around and lifted the mangled chair. It was only a further few minutes when someone with a first aid bag threw a blanket over the body.

Lydia made her way down the gantry and checking both ways, moved off towards the exit. In the distance the wail of an ambulance was getting louder.

CHAPTER FIVE

It had taken forty-five minutes to get back to her house in Acton from the Borehamwood ski complex. As she opened the front door she could hear the wailing and the panting. 'YES! YES! YES! OH GOD! YES!' Then the satisfied grunts as the lovers collapsed together.

Rick and Sandra were at it again. Rick must have waited until she'd gone and then brought the bitch back. The fucking nerve of the bastard. She knew she should have got her door key back. Too late now.

It sounded like they were in the lounge. Lydia crept towards the door and peered in. The television was on. Michael Douglas had Glenn Close sitting on the kitchen draining board with her legs wrapped around his waist in Fatal Attraction. With everything else on her mind she must have forgot to switch the TV off when she left earlier.

Picking up the handset she ended the film. However, she could still hear them. This time from the kitchen. They must have been watching the film and got all randy.

Lydia edged towards the door. The smelly remains of last night's fish and chip supper still lingered from the pedal bin. She knew she should have thrown it out.

She could clearly hear them again now. The banging on the sink top. 'YES! YES! YES! OH GOD! YES!' Then once more the satisfied grunts.

As Lydia reached the kitchen it went quiet. She made for the large chest freezer and lifted the lid. She smiled. Amongst the frozen peas and Birds Eye fish fingers the decapitated heads were attached in a frozen loving kiss. The hands and feet were neatly beside each owner in such a way that you couldn't see the nasty cut off ends.

Lydia smiled at them and closed the lid. At least she knew where they were now, instead of speculating. Was he humping her in his office after hours? Or a local Holiday Inn? Or back at her flat?

*

It was a couple of months ago she heard their moans from the ground floor hallway. 'YES! YES! YES! OH GOD! YES!' Then the satisfied grunts as the couple collapsed together.

Lydia had come back early from an unsuccessful audition and wasn't particularly in a good mood. Creeping up the stairs she spied her husband Rick and his secretary

Sandra through a crack in the door. It was then the anger inside her rose up like a red mist. She couldn't restrain herself. He fingers clenched as she watched them humping and moaning again. They had to be punished. It was only fair. Then she'd wipe the slate clean and forgive him.

As if in a trance, Lydia had quietly made her way down the stairs. She remembered the axe her husband used to chop wood for the outside pizza oven. Opening the door she saw it neatly sitting on the chopping block next to the oven.

Picking it up it felt heavy in her hand. Knowing the high fences either side gave her seclusion from the neighbours, Lydia tried a few practise swings. Then she came back in. With the axe by her side she made her way up the stairs again to the sounds of their lovemaking.

As she entered the bedroom he was on top with her legs wrapped around his waist.

The first blow struck her husband on the back of his skull. He half turned and then she struck him again. Rick rolled off his little tart twitching and moaning covered in blood. Sandra couldn't quite comprehend at first. She looked at lover boy in astonishment and then back up to her. That's when Lydia raised the axe as Sandra was about to scream.

The crunch of steel against bone stifled her cries. One more blow on each of their heads was enough to render them both a passage to eternity. The staring eyes and the gaping bloody mouths confirmed their departure from this world.

Now Lydia had to act fast. With no clothes on either of the bodies it made life a bit easier. She searched her husband's pockets and found the car keys to his Ford Focus. She didn't notice his car outside. Perhaps they'd come in just the one car, his secretary's. Lydia searched Sandra's shoulder bag and found her car and flat keys in a zipped compartment.

Changing into Sandra's clothes and a fancy dress party wig that could pass for the real thing, she took Sandra's car and drove to her flat late at night; stopping off at a twenty-four hour Tescos supermarket to buy a pair of plastic shower curtains and a self-catering holiday guide from the magazine and newspaper aisle.

As Lydia swung into the carpark adjacent to the block, she spotted her husband's car in one of the bays.

Using her husband's mobile phone and his contacts details, she phoned Sandra's flat to double check she lived alone. When no one picked up she let herself in.

Gathering all her clothes and jewellery, she stuffed them into two suitcases she'd found. Then Lydia tidied up the flat to look as though Sandra had gone on a planned holiday. She opened the holiday magazine to the page that stated 2016 Best Deal Holidays for Self-Catering and then circled in Biro numerous apartments in Cyprus and left it on the coffee table.

Lydia let herself out and returned to her house parking Sandra's car in her own garage. Although it was nearly one-thirty in the morning she didn't feel tired. There was too much adrenalin running through her. Lydia immediately set about gathering her husband's clothes and possessions and stuffed them into another two large suitcases.

Now came the grisly part. She carried two thick bed spreads into the bath tub. These would hopefully deaden the sound. Then with difficulty she dragged both bodies into the bathroom. Using all her strength she lifted the first body into the bath tub. With the axe she chopped off the head, hands and feet. Lydia did the same with the second body.

When she'd finally finished and had the torsos wrapped up in the blood sodden blankets, Lydia vomited into the sink. It had been a long time coming. She heaved a number of times more until she brought up bile and then rinsed her mouth out with water and a capful of Listerine.

With the torsos sealed up in the shower curtains using duct tape, she dragged them down the stairs and then out into the garage using the connecting kitchen side door. Struggling and cursing she hauled each one into the boot of Sandra's car. Then Lydia went back to double check. The only incriminating things left were the bloody blankets, the mattress and the suitcases. That meant a visit to the local refuse dump in the near future. Meanwhile, she had to get busy mopping down the blood spatters in the bedroom and bathroom. That would while away the hours until the morning. Lydia just hoped her run off husband and his floosy wouldn't arouse any suspicion involving her. She didn't want a forensic team going through her house spraying Luminol everywhere.

Catching just three hours sleep, Lydia showered and made herself some breakfast by early that Sunday morning. Looking out of the window she saw the weather was on her side. Although early July, the summer for 2016 could have been better and it was pouring with rain. That was good. The ground already softened up from previous downpours and the unkind weather keeping away dog walkers, ramblers and the odd strolling couple, would hopefully let her do her job of digging a hole for lover boy and his mistress.

By midday at Horsenden Hill Woods just off the Greenford Road, she was done. Lydia had been there a few times on days out with her ex to play golf at a local club. The woods were quite dense in places.

Using the shovel, Lydia patted down the slight mound and tossed away any excess earth. Then she covered it over with some loose branches she'd collected. In the pouring rain she stood for a while to admire her work. Hopefully nobody was going to find these two for a long time.

That Sunday lunchtime she'd joined the long queue of cars at her local rubbish tip. When her turn came, the garbage man dressed in a yellow sou'wester asked what she had.

Lydia responded, 'Oh, some old suitcases and blankets.'

He pointed to the landfill skip and let her through.

Lydia had to make three journeys by foot until the boot of her car and the back seat were empty. She even watched the crusher do its job. The steel piston with its massive plate pushing down the suitcases and then shoving everything to the rear of the container to make room for more rubbish.

Later that Sunday afternoon, using Sandra's car and wearing her clothes again, she took the M23 to Gatwick

Airport Long Stay Car Park, North Terminal. She arrived just before six o'clock at the barrier. Being July and the holiday season, the carpark was nearly full.

Looking around it was quiet as she paid cash at the pay on foot machine for a 90 day stay ticket. As the barrier lifted she chose a remote bay at the perimeter of the carpark.

With a handkerchief, Lydia wiped off all possible traces of prints and then, leaving the parking sticker in full view, she climbed out and instantly pulled down the big floppy hat she'd brought along. With an abundance of security cameras, she kept her head down as she made her way to Gatwick North Train Terminal.

CHAPTER SIX

It was two weeks later on a Friday evening that Lydia heard the doorbell chime. Two gentlemen on her doorstep showed their warrant cards.

A tall, stocky, fifty-three year old Detective Inspector Gordon Barnes with an early lined face and pointed features, sporting a short back and sides greying haircut said, 'Good evening. Are you Mrs Lydia Perkins?'

'Yes I am. Why?'

Wearing a sombre blue suit he replied. 'We'd like to ask you some questions concerning your husband Richard Huntly. We have him as reported missing along with his secretary, a Miss Sandra Swain. May we come in?'

'Oh my God. I didn't know. Yes of course.' She led them through into the lounge. 'Umm, please take a seat. Can I offer you both anything? A coffee or a —'

They both interrupted in unison, 'No thanks.'

Wearing a light brown suit, Detective Constable Ian Edwards, a tall young twenty-six year old with dark hair and clean good looks, took out his pad and pen while his superior opened his notebook and flicked a couple of pages.

The Inspector asked her. 'Is Perkins your maiden name? Or—'

'Yes. It's also my stage name. That's why I retained it. I'm an actress you see.'

'Ah, that explains.' He looked at his notebook. 'Mrs Perkins, you could tell us about the last time you saw your husband?'

Lydia took a seat opposite the sofa the detectives shared. 'Well, you see we're separated. Have been for over four months now. My husband moved out to live with his secretary. The last time he called round was to pick up his clothes and things.'

'And when was that?' The Inspector, well trained in behavioural response, looked for negative body language, her answers, the pitch of her voice and eye contact.

'Umm, about... a month ago.'

'Did he give you any indication of taking a holiday or moving away somewhere?' The Inspector noticed she glanced away at this question and held one arm tightly with her other hand.

'Umm. Come to think of it, now you say holiday. I saw a brochure with some other magazines and books in the hallway. He was getting ready to put them in his car boot.'

The Inspector replied, glancing at his Detective Constable. 'That might explain the holiday brochure we found in his secretary's flat.' The Inspector checked his notes. 'He never mentioned going to Cyprus? Some apartments there were ringed with biro in the brochure.' The Inspector watched her lean back at this question and cross her legs.

'No-no. He never mentioned to me. And then why should he?' Lydia mocked nervously. 'No doubt, he and his secretary are sunbathing themselves somewhere on some sun soaked beach.'

'It might look that way. However, we checked all recent flights with their details and even ferry sailings. It seems they never purchased any tickets or left the country.' The Inspector saw Lydia shift uncomfortably.

'Really.' Lydia coughed nervously to clear her throat.

Inspector Gordon Barnes became serious. 'Two days ago we found Sandra Swain's car in a long stay carpark at Gatwick Airport. CCTV shows only a woman leaving the car. Although the camera didn't reveal a good facial description, the clothes she was wearing match Sandra Swain's.'

Lydia relaxed. 'Well then, Inspector. Surely that shows you they must have met up somewhere and taken a flight.'

The Inspector studied her face. 'Not necessarily. It might have been someone in disguise to throw us off the scent.'

Lydia gripped her arm tighter and looked him straight in the face. 'What exactly are you trying to say, Inspector?'

'Mrs Perkins, are you aware, your husband as an accountant was embezzling the company he worked for? It appears with his secretary's help, he'd taken three-hundred thousand pounds from various client accounts.'

Lydia looked at him gobsmacked. 'You're joking me. He's stolen three-hundred thousand pounds?'

'Yes and we believe there was a third person involved.' The Inspector took out a photo and leant across to show her. 'This was taken by a CCTV camera four weeks ago at a HSBC Branch in London. It shows a woman masquerading as one of your husband's clients making a bank transfer to an account in Newton Abbot, Devon. The amount was for one hundred and fifty thousand pounds. Since then the account has been debited and closed.'

'Yes... So,' Lydia looked bewildered. 'Why are you telling me this?'

'You will see in the picture.' The Inspector pointed. 'Although the face isn't clear, the woman's hair pulled back and her clothes are similar to yours I believe?' The Inspector nodded to her framed photo on the coffee table taken with a similar hairstyle at an audition. 'The family picture of you and your husband that he kept on his office desk, confirms the similar clothes. Also, from our investigations, we discovered you once lived around the Newton Abbot area where the account was held.'

Lydia scoffed at the photo. 'We didn't split up the best of friends. He could be trying to frame me. Make me the patsy for his own crooked plans.' Lydia looked for a response from them. There was none forthcoming. 'Are you trying to imply, Inspector, I was involved with this?'

'We're not implying anything for the moment, Mrs Perkins, but you have to see it from our point of view why we have to follow up these enquires.' The Inspector paused. 'In saying that.' He made eye contact with his Detective Constable. 'Is it possible to have a look round while we're here? Or... would you rather us obtain a warrant first?'

Lydia stiffened. 'No-no by all means help yourselves. I've nothing to hide I can assure you.'

They both stood up. The Inspector asked her. 'If you would stay here while we have a look around I'd be most obliged.' He nodded for his Detective Constable to try the upstairs while he began to open the doors and drawers of a bookcase and then rummage through the books above. Then it was onto shelves filled with DVD's including checks behind the sofa and under the carpets. Then the Inspector moved into the kitchen.

Lydia heard worktop drawers and wall cabinet doors opening and closing. Knives and forks being rattled. Waste and pedal bin lids being flipped.

The chest freezer being opened.

Lydia froze like its contents. As long as he didn't dig down underneath the peas, pizzas and fish fingers.

She held her breath. It seemed an eternity, waiting for some sort of shout or alarm, but nothing. She heard the lid shut down.

Lydia breathed out and relaxed.

After a further five minutes they reappeared. The Detective Constable shook his head to the Inspector.

'As I said, Mrs Perkins, we have to follow a process of elimination and thank you for being most cooperative.'

Lydia walked them to the front door.

As they were leaving the Inspector turned and handed Lydia his card. 'If you think of anything that might be helpful or they contact you for any reason, please let us know. Any information by the public is treated in the strictest confidence.'

Closing the door behind them, Lydia collapsed back onto the wall with relief. Dear God, how lucky was that. She'd only restocked the freezer two days ago nearly to the brim. Who would have thought the police would be snooping around so soon because little old Rick and his ball of fluff had been found with their hands in the till.

A few days later, Lydia curled up on the sofa with a glass of wine. She pulled her list and ticked Dina Burlington. She remembered curvy Dina with her long platinum blonde hair and Nordic good looks. She was the bitch who beat her at the audition for the role of Nora in the Doll's House play. Lydia read the poem. *Second pretty actress driving as she sped. Then a life threatening car crash leaves her very dead.* She looked at her notes on Dina and the underlined. *Dina Burlington: Hobbies: Swimming and Go-Karting. An accident while driving a Ferrari around a racing circuit.*

*

A week later the postman called and asked Dina to sign for a parcel with a card. She double checked the name and address. It was hers alright.

Taking it into the kitchen she was like child at Christmas. Dina greedily ripped open the party paper and bubble wrap. She slowly held up the china doll dressed in a quaint Nora Helmer costume. She thought a while. Was it Fran her best friend? She looked at the hand writing. It didn't look like Fran's. What about her agent Maurice Weinstock. It could be from that old letch. Trying to soften her up. He'd made advances before. A dirty weekend in Brighton was the last. Not exactly Paris or Rome. No, this was too expensive for Maurice. Then she twigged the Dolls House connection. Perhaps it was someone from the cast. The producer or the director.

Dina opened the envelope. There was a congratulations card inside from *Favourite Days Out Ltd*. It took a minute to comprehend. The card finished off by stating in hand writing- Have a great day. Will be in touch next week. X

Dina couldn't believe her good fortune. She'd been Go-Karting many times, however, to win a day spent at Brands Hatch driving a Ferrari 458 Spider around the circuit with a trained driver was unbelievable.

Dina's enthusiasm for motor racing sometimes overflowed while driving her seven year old Mazda MX Sports, resulting in being booked for speeding on more than occasion.

Brian her live in boyfriend wasn't the jealous type. He only wished the event had been for two. Still he could take or leave watching motor racing. Too processional he often told her.

For Dina, Go-Karting and watching formula one were like a drug.

She tried to find out who'd arranged it, but the events company informed her they couldn't break their customer confidentiality. All they had been told, *the event was a present to Dina from a girlfriend admirer.*

Nine days later on arrival at Brands Hatch in the morning, Dina had to sign some insurance papers and waivers. Then wearing her one piece Kart suit with shoes, gloves and helmet, she spent the first couple of hours with her instructor on technique and steering skills.

At midday after a slap up lunch without alcohol in the club member's restaurant she was ready to spend the rest of the afternoon driving at over 125mph around the circuit.

A few days before, Lydia had staked out Brands Hatch circuit walking around its perimeter. The weather this late July had turned good. It was warm with clear skies and no wind.

During the night, she'd climbed a tree overhanging part of the Hailwood Hill Straight. She knew this was the stretch long enough for cars to build up speed before they went into Druids Bend.

Well hidden, Lydia made herself comfortable wearing a dark green track suit with trainers. She'd also brought along some sandwiches and a flask of coffee.

Lydia stretched out along the thick tree trunk. Using high powered binoculars she could see Dina getting into the red Ferrari 458 Spider with her racing instructor. Then they roared off.

Lydia waited for them to come round the first time. She had the front tyre in her sights and pretended to squeeze the trigger. She made an adjustment with a small screwdriver on the telescopic sight and then waited for them to come round again. This time she knew she had the correct focus for the crosshairs which were now dead centre on the leading Ferrari tyre.

Lydia held her breath, took aim and squeezed the trigger.

Suddenly there was a tremendous explosion as the Ferrari, travelling at 98 mph, spun out of control and somersaulted into the crash barrier and then flipped over and burst into flames. The track was littered with debris.

There was silence for a few seconds as thick black smoke curled upwards from the wreckage. And then all hell broke loose as sirens sounded off and a flood of emergency vehicles began racing to the scene.

Looking through her binoculars, Lydia could see the chemical fire extinguishers put out the billowing flames within seconds. However the fire crew, dressed in their bright yellow safety suits, had to cut free the two occupants from the mangled wreck.

Hosing down the burning bodies and then a quick check by the paramedics, it could be seen their injuries were too severe to have survived. Dina and her instructor were then laid out on the scorched tarmac and covered with a blanket.

Lydia smiled to herself as she saw the smoke of the crash still rising up in a fading black wispy column. She knew her work was done.

She waited a while and scanned the area with her binoculars. Making sure there was no one around, she climbed down from the tree. Then dismantling the rifle parts into a rucksack, she changed quickly into ramblers clothes. With a long walking stick and a map tucked under her arm, she made her way through a thick clutch of trees until she reached her car that she'd parked in a nearby lane.

It was quiet as she rested back in the car seat. Lydia felt exhausted. She checked her watch. It had just gone 3:30pm and this was her first chance to rest having been up all night.

Lydia fumbled in the glove compartment and brought out a small bottle of brandy. She unscrewed the top and took a swig. She winced at the initial burn and then felt the gradual warmth as it found its way. As she stared out of the windscreen her thoughts went back to her school days and the first time she'd tasted brandy with Ian in her bedroom.

CHAPTER SEVEN

Her old school located on the outskirts of Denbury in Devon was a mixed sex academic type consisting of a lower school and a sixth form. It was state run, non-fee paying, which pleased her parents. Unlike her older sister Caroline, who was having the benefit of a private education at a top boarding school in Exeter and then no doubt onto university.

However, Lydia felt she never fitted in. That was until as a fourteen year old she met Ian Holmes at Denbury High.

In 1996, Ian Holmes, a tall for his age good looking lad with fair hair, had just turned fifteen years old and was smitten by Lydia's good looks.

Lydia by now was medium height with frizzy dark hair and a hoisted up school uniform skirt. She knew she had Ian hooked.

They were in the same class together and became inseparable during breaks and lunchtimes.

While Lydia received some pocket money helping out on her parent's farm, Ian worked the odd Saturday in his father's grocery store in Denbury High Street. Now and again they would pool their resources and go to the cinema. One such film was the old classic Bonnie and Clyde. It made an impression on them. On the way home by bus they talked excitedly about how good it would be to rob a shop or even a bank. Lydia told Ian about her father's guns. However, they decided to start small with Jessops the local newsagents.

That was it. Always needing money for cigarettes and booze, they thought they'd chance their arm. Jessops on Denbury High Street seemed an easy score.

Old Mr Jessop, since his wife died, ran the shop on his own. The cigarettes were stacked at the rear of the counter, well out of reach of greedy young schoolkids' hands that used to swamp his shop mostly for candy and chocolate after school.

The plan was for Lydia to ask for sweets kept in the jars on the far opposite top shelf. While Mr Jessop, with his back to them, would climb his set of steps; Ian with his mother's shopping bag would help himself.

Mr Jessop took pride in his top shelf jars. They'd been handed down from his father and his father. Filled with mint humbugs, acid drops, sherbet lemons, pear drops, liquorice allsorts and numerous sweets of a bygone era, they mostly attracted the elderly that still had teeth and could chew.

This mid-July, Devon was experiencing a warm spell. It was too hot to go shopping. Most people this Saturday afternoon were either at the coast or sitting in their gardens. The high street was quiet as Lydia made her way into the empty shop. The door was open due to the good weather.

Mr Jessop, sitting behind the counter reading a newspaper, raised himself. He was dressed in his usual khaki work coat wearing a pair of half rim spectacles. The overhead shop light reflected off his bald patch as he smiled at her and said, 'Yes, my Dear?'

Lydia with her dark frizzy hair tied back and wearing a white skimpy blouse with matching shorts, pointed to the jars. 'A small cup of your sherbet lemons and the same with the liquorice allsorts please.' She gave Mr Jessop a broad smile.

'Certainly.' He returned the smile and picked up the small set of steps and moved to the far end wall with the jars above. Positioning the steps, he gingerly climbed up with the paper cup in one hand and carefully unscrewed the lid for the sherbet lemons.

Lydia ensuring there was no CCTV or wall mirror, beckoned Ian who quietly appeared wearing a hood and quickly started helping himself to five packets of Benson and Hedges, a box of matches and a small bottle of Napoleon brandy.

Within twenty seconds all was in his shopping bag and then he was gone, leaving Lydia staring at the back of Mr Jessop as he fulfilled her purchase requirements.

Five minutes later they met up at the bus stop along the high street. Both sucking on a sherbet lemon and inhaling deeply on a shared cigarette, they giggled at their first successful venture into the world of crime.

'Do you want to come back to my place? My parents have gone to the big farm show in Newton Abbot. They'll probably go on to eat so they won't arrive home till late.'

'Okay, sounds great.' Ian took out the brandy. 'We can have a party,' he grinned.

Within forty minutes, they'd taken the bus and then a quarter of a mile walk. Finally, in between a swig of brandy each, they arrived at Lydia's farm house.

Letting themselves in, she immediately said, 'Did you bring them with you?'

Ian took the packet of Durex from his top pocket.

'Good, let's go to my bedroom.'

*

While Ian had ensconced himself in the bathroom, Lydia undressed and slipped into bed. Knowing it was her first time she felt nervous. She'd let Ian breast fondle and done some pretty heavy petting with him, but that's as far as it had gone. However, Lydia had made her mind up to moan and gasp in all the right places to show she was enjoying it. She didn't want it getting back to his mates at school, Lydia Perkins was frigid.

When Ian came back out of the bathroom he had his underpants on. He gave Lydia an embarrassing smile and sat on the edge of the bed. In his hand he held the packet of Durex and took out a rubber. Then Ian began to read the instructions on the back.

Lydia saw the funny side and poked him in the ribs. 'Haven't you used one before?'

'Err, no.' He tried to act cool. 'Always rode bareback.'

Lydia prodded him again. 'You're a virgin aren't you, Ian? Come on, be honest.'

He flushed up. 'No-no, it's just... I'm not too sure how they fit.'

Lydia sat up and placed her hand on his crotch.

Ian stiffened automatically.

She swung her legs out of bed and sat next to him.

Ian held his breath. God she was beautiful. He looked at the little vee her pubic hair made and then her gorgeous little breasts.

Lydia helped him out of his underpants. 'Here, let me have a go.' She peeled open a rubber and then rolled it down over his erection.

They kissed and fondled each other. Lydia guided his hand down between her legs.

Ian stroked her and could feel she was wet.

Then she took the initiative and pulled him on top, guiding him inside her.

Within a minute and a half, while Lydia moaned and shrieked on cue, Ian shuddered to a grand halt and then slumped lifeless on top of her.

'Jesus. That was great,' he said. 'Was it good for you?'

She kissed him. 'That was fantastic. Let's lie back and smoke a cigarette like they do in the films.'

With his arm around her, Lydia felt complete. She wasn't a virgin anymore. She could join in the conversations at school now with the other girls when they bragged about getting laid. And at this moment in time, she loved Ian more than anything. She couldn't imagine life without him.

It was after they'd tried it again. A little more measured this time, Lydia said, 'I'm starving. Sex makes you hungry.' They both laughed and climbed out of bed and got dressed.

Downstairs they sat at the kitchen table devouring a thick wedge of game pie each and a Scotch egg in between slurps of brandy mixed with coke, all from the refrigerator.

Ian belched at which they both laughed and then he said, 'So where does yer Dad keep his gun?'

'In his strongbox out in the pantry.' Lydia confirmed turning serious. 'But that's out of bounds.'

'Oh, come on, Lyd', just a peak,' he pouted. 'Your Dad won't know.'

She thought for a second. 'Okay but you can't mess with it. Just a look and that's all.'

She knew where the spare key was kept. On top of the cupboard.

Unlocking the narrow steel door, made Ian gasp. 'Jesus, is this the real thing. Let me hold it, Lyd', please,'

'Okay, but that's all.' She lifted it out and handed it to him.

Ian raised the Remington 1100 shotgun to his shoulder and pretended to take aim. 'Wow this could do some damage.' He looked at the boxes of cartridge shells on the strongbox shelf. 'Any chance I could fire it outside, Lyd', just to see what it's like?'

'No chance. What if my parents came back? I'd really be in the shit.'

'You said they'd be back late. And you're always telling me how good you are with an air rifle at your gun club. Or was that just all talk,' Ian mocked.

Lydia defended herself. 'I am good,' she said all serious. 'Came third in the junior county close air rifle championships this year.'

'Did you now?' Ian picked up some cardboard targets from the shelf. 'Still reckon I could get nearer the bulls eye than you.'

Lydia scoffed. 'You, you've never fired a rifle before.'

'I tell you what, Miss Annie Oakley. I bet you a Kentucky fried meal tonight, using two bullets each, I can get nearer to the centre than you.'

Lydia corrected him. 'They're not single bullets you know, but lots of small lead shot.' She checked her wallet. She had a fiver and a one pound coin. Lydia looked up, 'Okay, Mr Wyatt Earp, you're on.'

Ian and Lydia went around the rear of the farmhouse out of sight from the road. In the three o'clock afternoon heat they set up a target pinned to the side of a barn. From it, Lydia measured fifty feet back and set down a matt.

'Okay. Let me fire first so you can see my stance and how my shoulder buffers the recoil. Or you could end up with a very sore shoulder sprain. And remember, in target shooting, don't pull just squeeze the trigger.'

Ian saluted her and joked, 'Yes Ma'am.'

She continued. 'Most important of all, when not firing, always carry it upright or over your shoulder. Never point it at anyone.'

He saluted again. 'Yes, Ma'am.'

Lydia sneered at him. 'You can joke, Mr Wyatt Earp, but we'll see how good you are.'

She loaded four 20-gauge shells into the tubular magazine and put on a pair of safety glasses and ear muffs.

Taking up the stance, she fired two off immediately.

Ian rubbed his ears. 'Jesus, Lyd', you looked like Bonnie doing a bank job.'

Lydia moved to the target. The centre was spattered with small led shot holes. She handed it to him. 'Now see if you can do better.'

'Wow, some shooting, Lyd'.'

With another target pinned up, Ian wearing the safety specs and earmuffs, took aim and then fired.' The instant recoil made him jerk back and he dropped the rifle uttering a loud profanity.

Lydia creased up laughing. 'Not bad, but I wouldn't hold a showdown with a top gunslinger at the moment.'

Ian picked up the rifle and unknowingly pointed it in her direction. 'Sorry, what did you say?'

Lydia froze and then reacted. *'UP!-UP!* Don't point.' Waving to him frantically. *'UP!-UP! Fuck sake!'*

Ian lifted the earmuffs with a puzzled expression. 'What did you say?'

Lydia crouched and moved towards him, gesticulating with her arms. *'UP!–UP! Point the bloody thing up!'*

Suddenly Ian realised. 'Oh, Jesus. I'm sorry.' He quickly raised the barrel as Lydia reached him and snatched the rifle out of his hands.'

'She bent over with sheer exhaustion and shook her head. 'Don't ever do that again, you, Dumb Fuck,' she shouted.

Ian playfully saluted and repeated, 'Yes, Ma'am, I mean no, Ma'am.'

Lydia, ejecting the last cartridge from the rifle magazine, saw the funny side and started to laugh.

He put his arm around her and joined in, mimicking. *'UP-UP' Point the bloody thing up!'*

That made her laugh even more and they both exploded into convulsive shrieks while she tried to say, 'You silly, Pratt! You could have killed me.'

With the rifle back in its strongbox and still early and hot that afternoon, they decided to take the bus to the fishing reservoirs near Newton Abbot on the River Teign. The Teign reservoirs were private and only accessible to fishing permit holders only. There was a warden who came round by van to check the permits from time to time, however, past experience showed that Sunday afternoons was his time off.

One reservoir very popular was Teigngrace with its overhanging trees where someone had tied a rope with a car tyre attached to it.

From the bus stop they took a short walk across a field until they reached the trodden down part of the perimeter fence; no doubt caused by non-permit holders, game poachers and teenagers like themselves that wanted to cool off.

On the bank they changed, Ian already wearing his trunks underneath and Lydia with her sexy cutaway thigh high one piece.

With no one else around, apart from a set of youngsters further down on the opposite side of the bank, they took the plunge and dived in. The water being deep enough at the very edge. Now with all the awkwardness out of the way they embraced and Lydia wrapped her legs around his waist while he doggy paddled.

A further twenty minutes later after embracing, kissing, punctuated by a lot of splashing and larking around, they clamoured to the bank. Checking their money, watches and mobiles were still safely hidden away under each pile of clothing, they climbed the tree with the swinging tyre.

After crawling out along the thick bough it was Ian who first slid down the rope and stood upright with his feet positioned on the inside rim of the car tyre. Then slowly working up a momentum, he generated a big swing and then leapt off with a loud Tarzan howl.

As Ian hit the water, Lydia heard a loud smack like a belly flop. She waited for him to reappear. As the seconds ticked by it seemed he was taking a long time. Lydia called out. 'Ian, stop messing around.' She crawled nearer to the dangling rope and shouted again. 'Ian, you okay? Ian fuck sake you're making me scared.'

Lydia hesitated. She was in two minds to crawl back down again or jump in. She scanned the water. She shouted again. 'Ian, you okay?' She waited a few seconds. 'Shit, if you're messing me around.' Lydia put on her goggles, took a deep breath, held her nose and jumped off.

She hit the water clean and nearly went to the bottom. Coming up she strained through her goggles but there was no sign of Ian. She doggy paddled and frantically shouted again. 'Ian, where are you?' She dived down again pulling herself as deep as possible while scanning the murky floor until she was about to burst for air. As she surfaced she gulped and coughed and felt sick. Lydia composed herself and then swam further out to have another go. Holding her breath she dived again, deeper still this time until her lungs were bursting. Still no sign of Ian. And the cold was getting to her. Lydia began to shiver.

She feverishly breast stroked her way to the bank and clamoured out. Then she ran to her clothes and found her mobile.

Pressing the buttons she panicked. 'Police, help me someone. My boyfriend's drowning. I can't find him.'

They responded and wanted to know details.

Lydia yelled. 'Yes, we're at the Teigngrace Reservoir. He dived in but there's no sign of him. I've tried to look myself.' With that she burst into tears.

*

Within five minutes the wail of an ambulance could be heard. Forty minutes later the area was crawling with police frogmen while Lydia, now dressed, was being comforted by a police woman.

For a further two hours, after refusing to be taken home, Lydia stood on the bank with a foil blanket around her shoulders drinking coffee as frogmen dived from rubber dinghy's and surfaced repeatedly.

It was then an arm raised itself from the inky waters with a shout.

Lydia approached the edge of the bank with the policewoman.

Two frogmen were holding something large. It was white. Then it was being hauled into the boat.

Lydia realised they'd all stopped and were edging their way to the bank. As the dinghy slowly motored nearer she had a horrible gut feeling. And then she saw the body bag.

The frogman reported the body was face down on the reservoir bed. He had to untangle the reeds around its ankles.

With the policewoman's hand on her shoulder, they unzipped the body-bag for identification. Ian's chalky white body stood out against the black frogman's rubber suit.

Lydia flinched back and began to sob uncontrollably. A few minutes later she watched the ambulance take him away to the mortuary.

Lydia dreamed of Ian that night. Trying to swim under the dark, reedy water to save him. In the murky distance he was ghostly white, waving to her. His eyes were upturned as though he was unconscious. The harder she swam the further he moved away.

CHAPTER EIGHT

A week later, after Lydia's statement at the Inquest, the Coroner gave a verdict of accidental death. The local newspapers had stated that Ian had drowned after hitting the water awkwardly and becoming disorientated as well as getting cramp.

On the day of the funeral, Mr and Mrs Holmes, Ian's parents, had his open coffin set out in their living room. Anyone was allowed to attend.

Lydia, dressed in her school uniform along with many classmates, clutched a white rose supplied by the parents. As they filed past they dropped the flower into the coffin.

The mortician had done a good job. It looked like Ian was asleep and there was colour in his cheeks, unlike the last time she had seen him. Lydia hovered before she dropped her rose. She wanted to touch him, wake him up.

Outside in the hallway Lydia sobbed along with some other classmates.

During a quiet moment, knowing their Ian was close to Lydia, the mother had retrieved Ian's Exeter City red and black football scarf from the coffin and gave it to her. Lydia promised herself she would cherish it for the rest of her life.

At the funeral, held in The Parish Church of St Mary the Virgin, every pew was filled to capacity with a video screen for the overflow of mourners outside. The service including a eulogy, was conducted by The Reverend Dr Kayhill along with tributes from Ian's schoolteacher and two of his friends. This was followed by the interment, at which Lydia couldn't watch. She was content to stare at the back of mourners and listen to the service.

For the next six weeks Lydia visited Ian's grave and knelt by the headstone talking to it. She'd saved up and brought along souvenirs from the Exeter FC club shop and laid out pendants and rosettes amongst the fresh flowers the parents replenished.

Gradually the visits became more infrequent as the memory of Ian, not unlike the red and black club colours of the mementoes she'd left, began to fade.

*

Lydia wiped away her tears and swigged the brandy again. She started the car and pulled out of the lane onto the M20. From there she would take the A20 past Swanley towards the South Circular Road onto Chiswick. From Chiswick a short drive home to Acton.

An hour and a half later she was letting herself in when she heard them again in the kitchen.

'YES! YES! YES! OH GOD! YES!' Then the satisfied grunts as they collapsed together.

Lydia lifted the freezer lid. The decapitated heads pulled away from their frozen kiss. Sandra looked up bleary eyed and then down into the white frost all embarrassed. Rick was feisty. He'd been drinking the most. The cap was off the Limoncello Liqueur. Some of it had slurped down their chins and settled at their neck stumps.

'Sho whadayer want Mish Nosey? Come to sheck up on ush again?'

Lydia smiled. 'I don't have to, Rick. I know where you are now. No more wondering whether you're working late or with your little tart. It's a lot off my mind I can tell you what with everything else going on.'

'Whadayer mean everyshing elshe going on. Ish can't be an audishion. Whoosh the fuck would give an audishion to a washed up hashbin drunk like yourshelfsh?'

Lydia responded. 'Now – now, Rick, don't get personal. Always know when you've had a drink. In fact it is an audition and a great part.'

Rick scoffed. *'Graysh Part? Don't shell me. Ish it for Godzshilla?'* Rick cackled away at his own joke while Sandra cringed.

'Now you're making yourself look silly, Rick, and embarrassing Sandra.'

Rick looked up at her with red drunken eyes. *'Fucksh shake you dull Old Cow. Carn't shoo shake a shoke. No shwonder I shleft you for Shandra. Shees gosh a sense of humour and shish besher in bed. Not cold and froshty like shyou.'*

'Cold and frosty, Rick. That's irony for you.' With a sarcastic laugh Lydia shut the freezer lid.

CHAPTER NINE

With her parents Saturday morning post still littered on the hall floor around her, she had taken delivery of a parcel with a fancy buff envelope stuck to it with her name *LINDA HARVEY* clearly written on the front in gold copper plate.

Linda opened the envelope and read the gold card. *CONGRATULATIONS LINDA. YOU HAVE BEEN GIVEN A FREE DAY OUT AT REIGATE AERODROME TO TRAIN AND FLY A MICROLIGHT AIRCRAFT WITH AN INSTRUCTOR. THIS IS CURTESY OF EXECUTIVE DAYS OUT LIMITED...*

Linda's eyes glazed over the rest. At the bottom it was signed *Have a great day. Will be in touch x.*

She'd done a bit of hand gliding and skydiving but this was unbelievable. Watching her nails, she tore open the parcel. It was a tin of ginger biscuits with a smiling ginger bread man on the lid. Linda stared at the card and the tin.

The first thing she did was to check out her parents.

In the kitchen her mother was rustling up breakfast. 'Not us, Darling. It's got to be one of your boyfriends.'

Her father looked up from his newspaper and shook his head.

Her mother suggested. 'What about that Derek you've been seeing?'

'I'm not seeing him regular.' Linda turned her nose up. 'Anyway I can't see him spending that sort of money. Especially when he asked me to go on holiday to Marbella with him and casually made it clear we'd go Dutch for the hotel and flight. At which I declined by telling him I was working on a new play.'

Spreading the toast her mother added. 'Then who do you reckon?'

Linda contemplated. 'It could be Jan or Carol. But they know it's not my birthday and we're nowhere near Christmas. And why the tin of biscuits? Christ! I don't even eat biscuits.'

By ten o'clock that morning, twenty-four year old Linda had showered and then squeezed her petite figure into a pair of tight hugging jeans and matching top, titivated with her ponytail and did her make-up. Linda knew she was pretty with her slight oriental features from her mother's side. She was always in work, whether it was modelling for catalogues, TV adverts or small theatre roles. Her most notable part was the lead in The Ginger Man. She'd received good reviews. However, with a limited run it never reached the West End.

Settling down at the telephone table in the hallway she was on the phone to Executive Days Out Limited.

'Hi, this is Linda Harvey. I've received a letter from you informing me I've been selected for a day out on a microlight aircraft for next Saturday at Reigate Aerodrome. Is this some mistake? I never ordered this. You may have sent it to the wrong Linda Harvey.'

The receptionist replied. 'Just one moment please.'

Linda heard a key board being tapped and then the rustling of papers.

'Hello, could I have your full name and postcode.'

'Yes. It's Linda Pauline Harvey at RM10 7EU.'

The receptionist queried. 'Is that forty-two, Torrington Road, Dagenham?'

'Yes.'

'Congratulations, you've been given as a present one of our executive days out to fly a flexwing trike microlight aircraft.'

'Are you sure? Who from?'

'Apparently it was paid for by a girlfriend of yours. She didn't say her name but told us she will be in touch with you later.'

'Really, that's amazing. She must have known I was into skydiving and parachuting.'

After the confirmation, Linda replaced the receiver. She stared at the gold ticket again and tried to think who it was. Being popular she had a number of girlfriends. The one that stood out was her best friend Jan. Jan knew she was into skydiving. She could ask her of course. But then it was supposed to be a surprise.

*

Getting ready that Saturday morning she had the television news on. It was showing the tragic ski lift accident. A picture came up of Tracey Dunne. Then a picture of the smashed up chair. A reporter said a full investigation of the ski lift was ongoing.

By ten o'clock that morning, wearing her red one piece sky dive suit and a crash helmet, Linda was sitting in a Flexiwing Trike two seater P&M Pegasus Microlight at Reigate Aerodrome. It was a perfect late July day for flying with a blue sky and a few white clouds and a temperature of 68 degrees.

The mid-thirties instructor called Brian spent an hour showing Linda the controls with her sitting in the front pilot seat. Then they went through safety first and the take-off procedure. Now sitting behind him, Linda listened as he read out in sequence a check of the mechanical gauges, instrument gauges, fuel tap, trim, wind speed and a visual 360 degree check for other aircraft. Satisfying himself, he powered up the Rotax 912 4-stroke engine and took the brake off. When they had reached 35 mph along the grass field, the instructor pushed the bar for lift and they began to climb at 200ft per minute up to an altitude of 1,200 feet.

Linda was exhilarated, it was a fantastic feeling flying at 60mph. Although she'd been up before in light aircraft for skydiving this was more open to the elements. The engine noise. The rush of wind. The collection of patchwork fields below. It must have been how the Wright brothers had felt on their first powered flight.

CHAPTER TEN

Lydia had positioned herself just outside the perimeter fence at Reigate Aerodrome. She'd parked her car off Crab Hill Lane and, dressed as a rambler with a rucksack, walkers stick, map and hiking boots, made her way by foot across a farm field.

Safe amongst a clutch of trees she'd seen Linda take off. She assembled her father's *Ruger 10/22 rifle* and followed the microlight aircraft in her telescopic sights. It was too far away at the moment. She had to wait until it circled round at a lower altitude when the low noise .22 hollow point shells would be their most effective at piercing the engine's critical components.

Lydia waited a further twenty-five minutes as the buzzing engine grew louder and then became visible. She could clearly see the microlight overhead.

As it began to descend on its flight path to Redhill Aerodrome, Lydia focused the telescopic sight.

Although Linda had two more flights planned for the event day, this was Lydia's only chance. Miss and she couldn't afford to stay out here and wait for them to take off again. It was too risky out here in the open.

With a small tree branch as a rest she took aim.

They had descended to just over one hundred and fifty feet when Lydia fired off two shots.

Suddenly there was a loud bang as the piston block was pierced. The rear engine instantly shut off and started smoking. Then came a burst of flames as fluid from a ruptured fuel line began spilling out over the hot engine block. It quickly became a moving ball of fire. Through the telescopic, Lydia could see them both. They were trying to beat out the flames as their flight suits became engulfed. In his panic the pilot had let go of the flexiwing steering bar.

Some aircraft maintenance people below were looking up. They pointed to the out of control spiralling microlight.

A few put a hand to their mouths in shock for the impending disaster.

With gathered momentum and traveling at around seventy-five miles per hour the microlight aircraft smashed to the ground and blew up in a rising ball of fire and black smoke.

Within seconds two aerodrome fire engines came racing to the rescue with flashing blue lights and wailing sirens. Firemen began unravelling hoses and started dousing the flames with fire suppression foam. The remaining white scene could have come from the front of a Christmas card.

The only difference being, the grisly remains concealed in the wreckage.

Lydia used her high powered binoculars. She could see no movement.

Satisfied she collected her things and made her way to the car.

*

Arriving back at her house she found the latest bank statement on the doormat. Walking through into the kitchen she lifted the freezer lid. Faint snoring was coming from both the heads. Rick and Sandra had finished off the bottle of Limoncello and no doubt were sleeping it off. She closed the lid and opened the bank statement. She was a hundred and fifty pounds overdrawn. That wasn't unusual. It was nearing the end of the month. Pay day was coming up just before the start of August.

She knew she was lucky to get the canteen job at AUTOMARTS LTD while resting, as they say in the showbiz world. With her savings gone, it filled a hole. A stop gap between paying the mortgage and bills or having to downsize.

While working in a factory canteen at the moment for a car auto parts manufacturer she'd had to negotiate her way around one of the security guards who'd caught her pilfering.

Because the wages were crap, the four other canteen women and herself would have a share out on a Friday afternoon unbeknown to the supervisor. Eggs, bacon, sausages, tinned baked beans, cheese, ham, pork and lamb chops were the favourite commodities as these were consumed and re-ordered on a weekly basis to provide the shop floor and offices with two tea breaks and lunch. Therefore difficult to stocktake at any time as these items were constantly coming in and moving out fast.

However, Lydia hadn't taken into account a short, overweight, balding, forty-eight year old night security guard named Aubrey.

Aubrey with his pig eyes and double chin fancied Lydia. He'd heard from the other canteen women she was single. Aubrey fancied his chances and knew what was going on.

He'd spotted Lydia with the others pilfering on the CCTV monitor he manned during the start of his evening shift.

This late Friday afternoon after tea break, they'd help themselves from the large walk in fridge-freezer. After the share-out, they'd carry the goods under their overalls to the cloak room and hide it in their lockers until the factory buzzer announced the end of the daytime shift.

This particular afternoon, Aubrey was waiting for her at the entrance of the ladies cloak room. He'd let the others pass and cornered Lydia on the pretence to have a chat. Aubrey being security, the other canteen women made themselves scarce very quickly.

Being laden down with her contraband she had to make herself amenable, while any other time she would have brushed him off.

Aubrey toyed with her. Asked if she would like to go on a date with him. He fingered the collar of her overall affectionately and told Lydia he liked the way she had her hair.

Lydia wanted to throw up, however, she maintained a coy smile and said maybe, hoping to keep him satisfied for the present until the goods were safely in her locker.

Then looking both ways to ensure they were alone, he wrenched her overall, tearing off two buttons as two packets of bacon, three packets of ham and two pounds of sausages fell to the floor.

Lydia's expression resembled a cat that had been caught licking the cream. She grinned inanely at Aubrey and said, 'Whoops!' Hoping his attraction for her would soften him up and let her go.

However, Aubrey the security guard was not amused. He pointed upwards to the CCTV camera and assured her. 'It's all been captured on film, Miss Perkins.' In a stern tone he made it clear. 'I'm afraid I will have to escort you to the managing director's office, Miss Perkins, and report what I've seen. The company has a zero tolerance on theft and the police will be called.'

Lydia being an actress and street wise, knew what to do. She burst into tears and sobbed. *'I'm sorry. Please don't tell anyone. I won't do it again, honest.'* With tears streaming down her face she grabbed Aubrey's hand and pleaded with him.

Aubrey smiled and said, 'Come – come now,' and patted her shoulder. He checked both ways and said, 'I'm sure we can work something out, Lydia.' With that he put his arm around her shoulders and slid his hand inside her overall and fondled her breast.

Lydia allowed him. She made it clear in-between further gulps and sobs. 'I'll do anything but please don't shop me.' While he continued to fondle her, she laid her head on his chest to show all was good and she didn't mind.

Aubrey was getting an erection. It didn't matter if he was a bit late on his security rounds. Soon everyone would be gone apart from the odd director working late. And their offices were on the other side of the building.

'I'm glad we can be friends, Lydia.' He kissed her fondly on the cheek. Aubrey's pig eyes wrinkled up as he grinned and suggested, 'We could both stay on late. I could meet you in the first aid room where it's quiet. They've got a couch there.' He became serious. 'That's of course if you want to?' Aubrey looked up to the CCTV camera and then back down to her.

Lydia read the alternative. 'Err, yes okay, Aubrey. Say around six-thirty when they've all gone. Give me time to freshen up in the ladies room, make myself available.' She smiled back and gave him a little peck on the cheek.

As they parted she noticed an unmistakeable bulge in his trousers.

Aubrey at the last minute turned and wrinkled his pig eyes again holding a finger to his lips. 'Remember, not a word to anyone.'

*

By six-thirty the cleaners, starting early on Fridays, had been and gone.

Lydia had sat in her Fiesta until the carpark was deserted. Checking her watch she took a last look in the rear windscreen mirror and climbed out. She made her way through the empty reception and using her canteen pass card, moved through the barrier which lead onto the factory floor. Lydia stopped first at the cleaner's cupboard and removed a broom and a duster. Then she made her way to the canteen.

Edging herself around the corner she looked up and could see the camera hovering over the walkway opposite the walk-in fridge-freezer. Out of its view she hoisted the broom handle with the duster on top and flipped it over the lens.

Aubrey had got himself ready in the first aid room. He'd taken off his jacket and was chilling on the couch. He was all excited. Besides a packet of DUREX he'd even brought along bottle of red wine with a screw top and two glasses from the canteen. And why not. Might as well have a glass or two before getting down to it he thought. And it should soften her up around the edges. Not like those hard slags under the railway bridge of a night. *All they wanted was yer thirty quid, the bitches.*

As Lydia arrived, Aubrey held his breath. In front of him she took off her blue work coat and let it slip to the floor. Lydia was wearing just a half cup bra with suspender belt and stockings.

Aubrey's pig eyes locked on to her panties as they lost themselves up the crack of her bottom. His hand instantly fondled his erection.

Her eyes lit up when she saw the bottle of wine. Lydia made herself comfortable on the first aid couch beside him. 'Are you going to drink that or keep it for Christmas?'

Aubrey lost in lust refocused his attention. 'Oh, I'm sorry.' He moved to the sink worktop and poured two glasses. He came and sat next to her and said, 'Here's to a long and lasting relationship.' His piggy eyes wrinkled up as he grinned and slurped his wine.

Lydia took a thoughtful sip and suggested. 'Do you know what, Aubrey? I'm starving. I could murder some cheese and biscuits with this wine. There's nothing worse than having sex on an empty stomach.'

He looked slightly puzzled. 'Where can we get that in here?'

Her face lit up. 'The canteen, of course. There's stacks of it in the fridge.' Lydia hesitated. 'Of course, you being security, I wouldn't want to get you into trouble.'

'No-no, don't be silly,' he scoffed. 'I can allow it this once.'

Lydia raised herself. 'I'll bring us back a couple of plates. Might as well if we're going to make an evening of it.' With that she embraced him and one hand went to his crotch.

Aubrey moaned with pleasure and his hands darted underneath her panty waist line and squeezed her buttocks. He was nearly bursting out of his trousers. He couldn't contain himself.

Lydia pulled away and slipped on her work coat. 'Now don't start without me, Mister Sexy,' she joked.

Aubrey looked longingly at her and felt himself again. 'Don't be long, will you,' he pleaded.

After she was gone he poured himself another glass of wine and sat on the couch.

Aubrey couldn't believe his luck. Compared to the slags that worked the patch under the railway bridge, Lydia was drop dead gorgeous. And she fancied him. He could see that. She couldn't keep her hands off him.

It was after five minutes he looked at his watch. Where the hell was she? For an instant it crossed his mind she'd done a runner. But that didn't make sense. She seemed dead keen and she knew he'd shop her for pilfering if she refused his advances. He had her on CCTV.

Aubrey moved off the couch and made his way out of first aid and proceeded along the factory gangway that hugged the wall. The canteen was at the far end through the lobby.

As Aubrey pushed open the swing doors the noise echoed through the quiet dining area. He made his way to the door with a sign stating KITCHEN – STAFF ONLY.

Aubrey tried the handle and it swung open. The stale smell of todays' lunch still lingered as he looked over to the walk-in fridge-freezer with its door open. As he approached he called out. 'Lydia – Lydia, where are you?' The interior was dark and Aubrey tried the outside light switch. He flipped it backwards and forwards and cursed. 'Bloody light,' he muttered. 'Probably the bulb.'

He called again. 'Lydia, where are you. Don't mess me about. The jokes getting thin.'

Aubrey moved inside the walk-in fridge-freezer and made his way to the rack that hid the wall behind. He peered round the shelves thinking she was going to surprise him and shout *Boo!*

Instead, Aubrey jumped at the sound of the fridge door as it slammed. He heard the bolt shot through and the padlock rattle its way into the hole as Lydia snapped it shut.

It was pitch black. Aubrey shouted out. 'Lydia, for fuck sake. The joke's over.' He felt for the shelves and made his way to the side, bumping into the worktops. 'Lydia open the door. It's pitch black.'

Inching his way along, he came to the door and banged on it. 'Lydia, open the door.' He felt for his mobile, it had a torch facility. 'Fuck it!' He remembered he'd left it in his jacket. Aubrey banged again and then felt a distinct chill. Was it getting cold in here or just his imagination?

In her Fiesta she smiled into the rear view mirror. They'd never used the fast freeze setting during work. Never had to because of the quick turnover of produce. Before fish fingers were half defrosted after delivery, they were under the grill during lunch times and on the plate with chips or mash and mushy peas as staff queued.

CHAPTER ELEVEN

Lydia made sure to be the first one in the next morning. She moved the switch from fast freeze back to the fridge setting and then, keeping out of view, she flipped the duster off the CCTV camera lens with the broom handle and then made herself scarce in the ladies toilet until the others arrived.

As Marlene the supervisor took the key from the kitchen drawer to unlock the fridge padlock to get the eggs, bacon and sausages for the early morning breakfast shift, the cold hit her face.

Aubrey was curled up frozen solid. It looked so surreal. She thought he was asleep until she poked and tried to wake him. Her shrill scream, '*Arrrrrh,*' brought the others running.

Marlene was in a terrible state. She blamed herself. Aubrey must have gone in there for some reason and passed out or had some seizure or heart attack behind the rack at the time she locked up.

Before the ambulance arrived it took over half an hour for the nurse in first aid to calm her down.

The police had the freezer switch checked out. It was old according to the service engineer and his report stated there were signs of electrical arcing. It possibly malfunctioned. However, the engineer replaced the switch with a new one.

CCTV revealed a temporary blackout. It sometimes happened that a camera went down because of a glitch in the circuitry.

The police after a thorough examination were quite satisfied no foul play was involved. This was later confirmed at the Coroner's Inquest for Aubrey with a verdict of accidental death.

*

Susan read the event invitation card again and opened up the Spanish fan. It had come in a decorative box. She tried to think who could have sent this. The day out at a clay pigeon shoot was a fantastic present. But from who? She had a birthday coming up in two months' time. A few of her girlfriends knew about it. Her best mate was Debbie. However, she couldn't ever remember telling Debs she was into skeet shooting let alone clay pigeon shooting. And she hadn't dated any guys since two months ago. And it wasn't her folks for sure. Christmas and birthdays she always received a Bodyshop basket from them.

She looked at the fan again. Had it been someone from the play? Nobody from the cast of Lady Windermere's Fan stood out and it had been four months now.

*

It had taken Susan Sinclair forty-five minutes from Enfield in Saturday M25 traffic to arrive at the Orion Clay Pigeon Shooting Club just off Chequers Road in Brentwood. The weather for the first week in August was fine again.

Having been skeet shooting for the last two years, twenty-eight year old, dark haired Susan with her Sigourney Weaver looks was dressed for the occasion. Wearing a pair of green mole skin jeans with a matching fleece and wax jacket, she finished off her countryside image with a Balmoral flat cap, tweed socks and leather boots. Not forgetting her ear plugs and Deben shooting glasses in her shoulder bag.

As she made her way to the club reception cabin, a tall young man dressed in similar shooting attire greeted her at the door. Susan handed him her event ticket and waited while he checked the details. With a smile he introduced himself as Steve and informed her he would be the coach for the day. Then he led her around to the rear of the cabin where she met David, Roger and Sally, the other people booked on the event with her.

At the end of a long wooden table, no doubt used for club BBQ's and picnics in the summer, sat a coffee pot with a plate of biscuits. Susan with the others helped themselves and made introductory conversation. From this, Susan learnt that Roger was also a shooting enthusiast while it was a first time for Dave and Sally. This could be seen by Dave and Sally's choice of clothes while Roger's outfit conveyed an outdoor shooting man wearing subtle colours that blended with the countryside.

Steve the coach handed them an Itinerary for the day and suggested they start on safety rules first and then how to hold a rifle and positioning while shooting.

Drawing them aside, he did apologise to Susan and Roger and was grateful for their patience while the other two as novices had to be taught the basics for the first part of the session.

Later that morning, holding Browning Cynergy CX over and under shotguns, they practised at paper targets using single shot on a firing range and then broke for a midday lunch.

The organizers had done them proud with a hot buffet mixture of English, Chinese and Mexican with vegetarian requirements.

In the afternoon it was decided to split into two teams for a competition clay pigeon shoot. It would be the men verses the women. This was fair, with an experienced shooter in each team.

With the two men on one side and the two women on the other, they took their places around the marked semicircle in the field.

At the shout of pull using cartridges filled with lead shot, each in turn wearing ear plugs fired at the clay targets being catapulted into the air from the release housings at opposite ends of the large semicircle. Out of four clays each, Susan and Roger scored a hit for their respective teams. This continued for another hour and a half with more advice and tips from the coach amongst some light hearted teasing banter from both sides.

With the women leading on the scoreboard they broke again for tea. This time it was a finger buffet of smoked salmon, chicken legs, sausage rolls, scotch eggs and quiche Lorraine with savoury tarts.

Around four o'clock in the afternoon, the two teams took their places again in the field semicircle and continued the competition. Then all of a sudden a small explosion over in the distance stopped everyone. It seemed to come from the perimeter of the woods and was followed by billowing smoke.

Steve used his binoculars and surmised it could be kids playing around with fireworks. 'Now they're sold all year round it's no wonder more injuries and small fires occur. And this late hot summer doesn't help, the dry bush is like tinder,' he informed everyone.

With the coach grabbing a fire extinguisher and the men holding a water bucket each, they left the women and moved over to where the fire had reduced to a thin curl of smoke. While Susan and Sally looked on holding their rifles, the men had disappeared amongst a clutch of trees.

Then a voice called in the distance. 'Susan.'

Susan heard it first. Someone was calling her name.

'Susan.'

Her head jerked a second time.

A hand went up and waved to her.

She couldn't see who it was, just the green sleeve of an arm waving. It was on the perimeter of the woods but away from the fire.

The person called again. 'Susan, it's Steve, over here,' and beckoned her to come.

Sally said to her, 'Looks like you're wanted to help out.'

Susan eyed her shoulder bag on the grass containing car keys, mobile and a purse with credit cards.

Sally saw her hesitate. 'Don't worry, Sue. I'll stay here and keep an eye on things.' Holding her gun she joked. 'I'll even stand guard.'

They both laughed and Susan thanked her and moved off to where the arm was waving.

At about fifty yards, Susan reached a hedgerow and found a stile to cross over. She heard her name called again and still couldn't see anybody. Susan shouted out, 'Where are you, Steve?'

She started to clamber over the style. Looking down she saw the step board the other side had rotted through. It looked too risky to put any weight on it without breaking an ankle.

The only choice was to jump down. Susan picked her spot and leapt off.

As her feet hit the ground there was the sound of a metal snap and then 'AARRGH!'

Susan screamed with the searing pain. Her foot was caught in a large animal trap. It had been buried just under the loose earth and leaves. The spiky clamps had smashed her ankle. Breathing in, trying not to pass out with the pain, she stooped and tried to pull the clamps apart. She yelled again. *'Fuck sake. Somebody help me!'* Just then she heard a voice from behind her.

Lydia calmly said, 'Oh my, God! Don't struggle with it. It'll only make it worse.'

Susan turned. 'Jesus Christ, Thank God.' In her pain she hadn't recognised Lydia. She bellowed again. *'AARRGH! The things agony. Get help. It's too stiff to move.'*

Lydia picked up the Browning Cynergy CX rifle that Susan had dropped. She checked the magazine. There was one up the spout. She'd brought some along just in case, but it didn't matter now. Lydia raised the rifle. 'I took a gamble on where you would jump. And it paid off.'

Susan on one knee, her vision blurred with the agonising pain, didn't comprehend. She murmured. 'What...what do mean?'

'The competition, Darling. We were down for the same audition. And there's only one part up for grabs on that TV sitcom.'

Susan now realised. 'You did all...' The pain was making her feel dizzy. 'You did all this... to get a TV part?' She breathed in deeply again and sneered. 'You'll never get... you'll never get away with it.'

'My dear, Susan, like all good scripts it's been thought through. You stepped on a poacher's animal trap, dropping the gun and it accidently went off in your face.'

Lydia took aim and squeezed the trigger.

Again wearing her rambler's attire with a walker's stick, rucksack and a map tucked under her arm, Lydia made her way from the shooting club across Weald Brook Woods. Coming out into the clearing she could see her car parked off the little lane hidden by tall scrub and bushes.

Lydia climbed into her Fiesta and went for the brandy in the glove compartment. She took a swig and closed her eyes. The rotted wooden style was a gamble. The Bitch could have thought it too risky. Moved along the hedge to get across somewhere else. However, the steel poachers trap did its job. The idea from the film *Kind Hearts and Coronets* had inspired her.

Although that wasn't the only time she'd seen a poachers trap snap shut.

CHAPTER TWELVE

She remembered Bess her black cocker spaniel. Abby the mother was her parent's farm dog. She'd given litter to six pups and Lydia at twelve years old had fallen in love with the only black one. She'd named it Bess after Dick Turpin's horse. While the other pups were advertised in the Farmers Weekly, Lydia was allowed to keep her Bess.

With her older sister Caroline at boarding school, Bess was the only real company she had. It was the first time that Lydia had experienced any natural affection. The puppy was all over her. Licking, nosing her face. They'd cuddle up together in bed although she had her basket. Before and after school Bess never left her side.

It was when Bess was six months old that Lydia and her father had started taking her on wood pigeon shoots on their Devonshire farm in Denbury. Bess was a quick learner and whenever she came back with a pigeon in her mouth she got rewarded with her favourite, chicken flavoured dog biscuits.

That morning they'd gone shooting early at 7.30am after breakfast leaving her mother in the kitchen potting jam for their farm shop.

Early morning for wood pigeon was the best time as the birds would come down from the trees to feed on the ground.

Her father was using his Remington 1100 shotgun with lead shot cartridges. At this stage of training they would throw a tennis ball into the forest shrub and Bess would go to retrieve it. Any pigeons would fly up at the disturbance and get picked off. It seemed to work every time with enough birds for a midweek casserole or for Sunday lunch with three or four set out on the dining table with red current-jelly and roast potatoes.

That early May Sunday morning, Lydia and her father had made their way into Denbury woods near the hill fort. They kept within the wire fence that marked the perimeter of her father's land. The woods here were quite dense. An ideal spot for pigeons to fly down and feed without the fear of being attacked by sparrow hawks. All they had to contend with was the odd fox that might creep up. Her father keeping chickens was well aware of Mr Fox. After numerous attacks on his hen coops he'd laid traps and baited them from time to time. The fox problem over the last few years had dropped off with so many becoming urbanised and preferring to rummage through bin liners and dustbins rather than take a chance with traps, farmers' dogs and shotguns. So he'd collected the traps up, so he thought.

At a spot they'd used before, Lydia and her father knelt on one knee. It was quiet, apart from a couple of woodpeckers working away and the rasp of the odd magpie.

With Bess by their side, her father showed the dog the yellow tennis ball. Bess became excited and started wagging her tail. Then with a big heave he tossed it into the far undergrowth.

Immediately the forest silence was shattered with a flurry of birds rising up with Bess chasing the tennis ball. Her father already on his feet fired off two rounds. Two pigeons came hurtling to the ground. Bess knew her training. She dropped the ball and went for the downed pigeons. It was then a terrible screech rose up and then a pitiful whimpering. The pair of them looked at each other. It couldn't be a pigeon. They don't make that sound. Lydia knew instantly something was wrong. She began calling for Bess. 'Bess. Come on, Bess, over here.'

As they began to walk towards the chilling whimpering sound, Lydia's stomach was churning. She started calling again. Becoming more anxious.

And then they saw her. Lydia screamed and rushed forward. She crouched at her pup. Both of its little front feet all mangled up in the fox trap.

Lydia began shouting at her father to free it. The pup tried to raise its head while Lydia pulled at the spiked clamp. She screamed at her father again to help her. It was too stiff to move.

It was then he started pulling her away. Telling her it was too late. Nothing could be done.

He began to reload his rifle.

Lydia sensed what was going to happen. She started pleading with him. *'Please don't, Dad. I beg you. We can still save her. Take Bess to a vet.'*

He father wasn't listening. He raised his rifle.

Suddenly Lydia dropped to her knees and grabbed her father around the waist in desperation. She pleaded again. *'Please, Dad, don't. Not my Bess.'*

He tried to push her away and shouted. 'Get off me, you silly bitch.'

Lydia began punching him. Shouting at him to stop.

Amongst the cries and blows, he coolly raised his twelve bore while she sobbed beneath him.

The blast made her stop. Then her anger took hold. Even at that age the red mist had descended. She looked at her dog and then back at him. 'You fucking, bastard. It was the only thing that ever loved me, and you killed it.'

He yelled back at her. 'It was the best thing for her, you dumb idiot. I'll buy you another one.'

'I don't want another one.' She screamed at him with tears and snot running down her face. 'I want my Bess.' On her hands and knees she crawled to the dog and buried her face in the bloody remains.

Her father dropped the gun and tried to pull her off.

Lydia gritted her teeth and held on.

'Come on, Lydia.' He had her by the collar. 'It's in a better place now.'

She turned to look at him.

Her father stopped. Let go and took a step back.

Her face was covered in blood.

He put his hand out to calm her. 'It's...it's Okay, it's...okay, Lydia. You're upset. We'll get you home and you can rest.'

It was then she made a grab for his rifle on the ground.

He realised and went for it too late.

Lydia levelled it at him. She started to laugh. A hysterical laugh.

He backed off. 'Put it down, Lydia. You don't want to do anything silly.' He was thinking. When he reloaded for that fucking dog. Did he put two in or just the one?'

She was holding the rifle in line with his chest and laughing in an unhinged way. 'You fucking puppy killer.'

He backed further away. 'Lydia, sweet heart. Let's talk this through. Just put the gun down.'

'Why should I, you bastard. You and mother never loved me. I was tolerated like your farmyard animals. I was adopted and raised so as to work the farm. That's all you cared about, your fucking farm and that lazy cow sister of mine.'

Jesus, he'd never seen the ungrateful bitch like this. It frightened him. He held both hands up to pacify her. 'Look, sweet heart. I know your mother and me don't always show our feelings. But that doesn't mean to say we don't love you. I take you shooting don't I? We go to the gun club and practise together.'

The red mist was beginning to clear. She lowered the gun and laid it on the floor.

Her father immediately grabbed it and checked the magazine. It was empty. He closed his eyes and breathed a sigh of relief. Then he went to strike her. *'You, stupid bitch! Don't ever point a gun at anybody again.'*

Lydia on the ground flinched as he lunged at her.

Her father stopped himself just in time. He thought better of it. 'Come on, let's go home. You go on. I'll bury the dog. Not a word about this. We'll just say Bess got caught in a poachers trap. Badly injured. We had to put her down there and then.'

Lydia stood up. 'I'm sorry, Dad.' She burst into tears and hugged him. He stood there, cold. His arms by his side. He didn't reciprocate.

Lydia pretended not to notice. She moved away. 'See you back home,' she mumbled and then made her way to the farmhouse.

CHAPTER THIRTEEN

A week later in the office of theatrical agent Maurice Weinstock the buzzer sounded.

'Yes Mary?'

'Mr Weinstock, there are two gentlemen to see you.'

The agent replied through the intercom. 'Show them in, Mary.'

Detective Inspector Gordon Barnes and Detective Constable Ian Edwards introduced themselves with their warrant cards and took a seat at the offered chairs.

Wearing a dark blue suit and matching waist coat, Maurice Weinstock's short, overweight, torso wriggled uncomfortably in his leather backed chair.

He was slightly nervous. His income tax returns hadn't been exactly truthful. However, if they spotted inconsistences his excuse would be his accountant had been ill and he wasn't a paperwork person.

The fifty-three year old Detective Inspector informed him. 'Mr Weinstock, we're here concerning the death of a Miss Susan Sinclair. I believe she was an actress and a client on your books?'

The agent looked astonished. 'My God, Susan Sinclair. Dead? What happened?'

'During a clay pigeon shoot she was killed. To begin with it looked like an accident, similar to the unfortunate deaths of the other three actresses on your books.'

'The other three, you're kidding me?' The agent sat up in his leather chair. 'Who were they?'

Detective Inspector Gordon Barnes nodded to his Detective Constable.

The young DC took out his notepad. 'Tracey Dunne died when the ski lift she was on broke away from the cable. Dina Burlington died in a racing car crash while being driven in a Ferrari and Linda Harvey died in an air crash while flying as a passenger in a microlight aircraft.'

'Jesus. That's a bit coincidental.' The agent sat back looking stunned. 'Now I remember seeing on the TV news. A skiing accident involving a Tracy somebody. But I didn't put it together. Dear God, you're saying all four actress's dead?' The agent thought for a second and then said, 'Surely there must be a connection?'

'You would think so, Mr Weinstock.' The DI squeezed his chin thoughtfully. 'Still, we've had forensic teams climb over the crash sites at the first three accidents and found no foul play. From the evidence of each crash, a plausible reason had been discovered. However, with Susan Sinclair's death we found anomalies. The gunshot wound was not consistent with the scene of the accident.'

The agent looked dumfounded. 'By what way?'

The DI explained. 'It initially looked like Susan Sinclair stepped on a poachers trap and at the same time dropping her rifle which instantly shot her in the face and killed her. The safety catch was off. Then further examination revealed the trajectory of the blast could not have come from ground level as when the rifle was dropped. It would have caused a wound from a bullet entering the body in an upward trajectory. Susan Sinclair's bullet wound had a downward trajectory. Which means she was shot while on the ground or kneeling when snared in the trap. Which means somebody else must have killed her.'

'Dear God. But who would want to—?'

The DI cut the agent short. 'That's why we're here, Sir. Perhaps you can help us with our enquires? Is there any one you can think of that had a grudge against her?'

The agent looked mystified. 'Well no, not really. I mean, there's always a bit of healthy competition at auditions for a good part. In fact all four of them were down to audition soon for a main lead in a television sitcom. If successful it would have furthered their careers no end with a handsome salary. However, I've never heard of or seen any hostility between artists that has led to a serious confrontation.'

The DI made a note and then asked. 'In the times you saw her, did she ever mention boyfriend trouble?'

The agent shook his head. 'No, can't say she did. I know she was married and then divorced.'

The DI nodded knowingly. 'Yes we've spoken to her ex-husband. He's been in Canada on business for the last three months.'

At that moment Maurice Weinstock had remembered the list of actresses for the audition in his desk drawer. He was about to show the two officers and then thought twice about it. The production casting director had only dealt with him. They were the only ones up for the TV part and now four were dead.

Suddenly a picture of thirty-four year old brunette Lydia Perkins with her sharp photogenic high cheek bones and tall slim figure, flashed through the agents mind. He'd remembered thinking, Lydia had that look of desperation about her the last couple times she'd been to his office. The look of desperation of someone who needed to work, and he'd told her she'd be up against stiff competition for that TV part. He knew his mind was racing. No, it couldn't be a woman? To kill for a TV part? And now it looked for certain she would get the role and hopefully he would get his fat commission. So it would be best all round to keep quiet about Lydia.

Then the agent remembered something else he'd seen on facebook.

The DI became serious. 'You see, Mr Weinstock, so far, you're the only person who has a connection with the four dead actresses including one suspected of being a victim of foul play. Wouldn't you say that's a coincidence?'

Maurice Weinstock straightened himself in the chair. 'Are you implying, Inspector, I had something to do with their deaths? If you are, it wouldn't make business sense on my part. I wouldn't bite the hand that feeds me. I get my commission when they're working.

At that, the DI nodded to his DC and they both stood up.

'Thank you for your help, Mr Weinstock.' The DI gave him his card. 'We will be in touch and if there's anything else you can think of, you can contact me on the card.'

After his secretary had shown out the two detectives, Maurice Weinstock immediately clicked on his facebook app and began searching.

*

Two months later, Lydia was over the moon. Her big break at last. With the main competition dead she attended the audition and landed the TV sitcom part. The initial pilot episode was a success with good reviews and now she had signed for a six episode deal with the TV network. For Lydia the money had started rolling in at last. She started to pay off her gambling debts.

And then one morning she received a letter in the mail.

Tearing it open, her hand suddenly froze. It showed a photo of herself with Susan Sinclair holding their prizes. Lydia remembered taking it on her iPhone at Battersea Funfair last year on the duck shooting stall. They'd both won small teddy bears at the same time and then got talking.

Being actresses they had something in common. Lydia had forgotten all about it. She'd uploaded it onto facebook. She'd assumed by now the photo would be buried deep within the facebook archive.

The accompanying letter was from her agent Maurice Weinstock. He wanted to see her the following evening at nine o'clock in his office to discuss things. Lydia guessed he wanted it quiet, out of hours with his secretary not there. No doubt, now she was in the money he wanted more of a share.

She'd come by train in disguise. A large blue hat and matching scarf hid her from street and local CCTV. As she pressed the buzzer, the shared business front door opened and she made her way up the flight of stairs. At his glass panelled door stencilled with **Theatrical Agent: Maurice Weinstock**, Lydia knocked.

'Come in.' Maurice looked up from his desk wearing a smart pin striped suit and smiled. He had Lydia's contract in front of him. 'Nice to see you again. Please take a seat, Lydia.'

She took a chair and removed her floppy hat and scarf.

From inside the contract he took a photo and pushed it to her across his desk. It was the same photo of Lydia and Susan Sinclair together. 'For reasons now apparent, I have amended your contract. All you have to do is sign and date where I've marked with crosses.' He slid the contract to her.

Lydia took a few seconds as she scanned the page and then said in astonishment, 'My God. You're taking fifty percent in commission?'

'A fair price, Lydia, considering. It's that or a lifetime behind bars. It would only take the photo with a letter to the police explaining your audition connection with the others. Especially Susan Sinclair. You never changed your old facebook details. What was it you had in common with her besides drama?' Maurice leaned in to his computer screen and adjusted his glasses. 'It says here on your facebook page, clay pigeon shooting. Now there's a coincidence.'

Lydia looked at him defiantly. 'That still doesn't prove anything.'

Maurice sneered. 'I'm sure if the police dug down deep enough they'd come up with something. For instance, you and your late father's connection with guns.' With that he slid out a newspaper clipping and pushed it to her.

Lydia stared at the headline. **DAUGHTER SHOOTS FAMILY AND THEN KILLS HERSELF.**

'It says in the column, you and your father shared a passion for guns. And after the tragedy you as the adopted daughter inherited everything. How convenient.' Maurice took out his pen and offered it to her. 'It seems, Lydia, people around you have died. Too many to be a coincidence, including that missing husband of yours and the money he'd taken.' He slid across the news item. **ACCOUNTANT AND HIS SECRETARY RUN OFF WITH CLIENTS' FUNDS**. 'With the letter and clippings to point them in your direction, I'm sure the police would refocus their attention on you. Attention you can ill afford.'

Lydia mocked. 'My, we have been the little Sherlock Holmes doing our research.' She declined his pen. 'It's okay, I'll use my own.'

Lydia half turned away and pretended to fiddle inside her pocket. Then suddenly she swung round holding her father's Ruger Mark III .22 semi-automatic pistol. She moved swiftly to Maurice. As he leant back terrified, she pressed the gun against his temple.

'What're you going to do? Don't be stupid, Lydia. You'll never get away with it.'

'On the contrary, you'll leave a suicide message on your computer admitting to the killings because the actresses spurned your advances. Knowing two of them were also going to report you for indecent assault, you couldn't live with yourself. The shame. The humiliation.'

Lydia opened his desk drawer and pulled out the diabetic insulin kit. 'Fill the needle to its 2.5 ml capacity.' She pressed the gun.

'Lydia, we can talk about this.'

She pressed the gun firmer at his temple.

Maurice's fingers twitched as he nervously tore open the package. Then he pierced the stopper of the insulin bottle and watched as the needle sucked up greedily to full capacity. 'Now you have a choice, Maurice.' Lydia pressed the gun. 'A bullet in the head that nobody will hear or an overdose. Bearing in mind I've only got one bullet. So I could miss leaving you paralyzed, even like a vegetable.'

Maurice began to whine. 'Please, Lydia. We can work this out. I promise I won't say anything. I don't even want any commission. It's all yours. Tear everything up.'

With the gun against his temple, Lydia stroked his forehead tenderly. 'The problem is, Maurice, you got greedy and started punching way above your weight. It's too late now.' Lydia clicked off the safety catch.

Maurice pleaded, 'Okay-okay.' He pushed up his jacket sleeve and clenched his fist. Maurice pleaded again. 'Please, Lydia. Don't make me do this.'

Lydia pressed the gun.

Maurice winced as the needle pierced. And then with his hand shaking, he pushed the plunger slowly down, administering the insulin.

Maurice relaxed. He seemed relieved. He sat there staring into space.

Lydia moved away and took her seat.

It didn't take long. Maurice began to mumble incoherently as hypoglycaemia began to set in. He began to shake his head from side to side. He began drooling. White frothy drool began oozing down his chin. His breathing started to labour until he was gasping. And then he tried to stand, gasping heavy, holding his chest in pain. Finally, his whole body shook with a final convulsive seizure and he collapsed on to his desk.

Lydia waited a couple of minutes and then checked his pulse. With him dead, she deleted the facebook photo of her and Susan on his computer. Then she checked his pictures file and deleted the same photo. Lydia did a file search using her name and found her details on his client list. She deleted this as well. Clicking on Microsoft Word, she typed his suicide message. Then Lydia went through his desk drawers and found the incriminating audition list. Last of all she went through his pockets and found his diary with copies of the photo and news clippings. Lydia pocketed these and carefully tore out the diary page with her contact details. She cast one last glance and remembered. The photo frame on the desk with the poem. She tucked it safely in her bag.

Double checking all was good and nothing out of place, she put on her floppy hat and scarf.

Within twenty minutes, Lydia was on the late night train heading for Acton Town Station.

CHAPTER FOURTEEN

Getting back late that evening she heard them again. Opening the front door, Lydia could hear the wailing and the panting. 'YES! YES! YES! OH GOD! YES!' Then the satisfied grunts as the couple collapsed together.

Rick and Sandra were at it again. No doubt on top of the kitchen sink, *Fatal Attraction* style. It was Rick and Sandra's favourite position. They must have waited until she'd gone out. The nerve of it.

Lydia crept towards the kitchen door and listened. She could hear them whispering and giggling. Her name was mentioned and then came laughing. They were mocking her. To think she'd given them a roof over their heads and this was the way they repaid her.

Lydia tensed with anger. She clenched her fists. The whispering and giggling continued.

Under her breath she cursed them. 'I'll show you two who has the last laugh. You want to take the piss out of me. I'll make you sorry.'

She took out the Ruger pistol. There was five in the magazine. She'd lied to Maurice.

Bracing herself, she cocked the gun ready and then lunged into the kitchen.

It was quiet. Lydia shouted, *'I know you're hiding. Come on out. All the exits are covered.'*

Lydia listened. Stifled laughing was coming from the freezer. Then she remembered.

She moved slowly towards it. As she lifted the lid it suddenly stopped.

Amongst the frozen peas and fish fingers the heads were still attached by the lips in a frozen loving kiss. The hands and feet were just the same, neatly beside each owner, protruding through the white frost in such a way, you couldn't see the nasty cut off ends.

*

It had gone 11:30 p.m. Lydia settled down with a glass of white wine on the sofa and switched on the TV for the late night film. She glanced at the photo frame on the side table. She idly recited the words. 'Five pretty actresses at an audition on a call. However, one sits alone and plots the others tragic downfall.

'First pretty actress learning how to ski, when suddenly she comes a cropper and gets injured fatally.

'Second pretty actress driving as she sped. Then a life threatening car crash leaves her very dead.

'Third pretty actress flying in the sky. When her aeroplane malfunctions, she knows she has to die.

'Fourth pretty actress who's shooting skill is ace. Then a gun goes off she's using and blasts her in the face.

'Fifth pretty actress, depressed at what she's done. Holds a pistol to her head and pulls the trigger of a gun.'

Lydia jerked and sat up. That wasn't the last line. 'I can't believe...,' she said to herself. 'Some one's changed it.'

'Well are you depressed?' Rick looked at her expectantly from the lounge doorway.

Lydia turned to the voice.

He was naked looking slightly green with a large gash in his forehead and dried blood around his neck, wrists and ankles. In his hand he held her Ruger Mark III .22 semi-automatic pistol.

As he approached, she flinched back in shock. Lydia put a hand to her nose. Rick was thawing out. The stench was foul.

He was by her side now. Lydia cringed away, there was nothing she could do.

Rick pressed the pistol to her temple.

CHAPTER FIFTEEN

It was the smell that first alerted the postman. By the time the police had broken the door down the place was crawling with flies and maggots.

Detective Inspector Gordon Barnes and Detective Constable Ian Edwards were the first ones at the scene. They found the suicide note sitting neatly on the coffee table. Wearing his sombre blue suit and with a handkerchief at his nose the DI picked it up with tweezers.

As he read the full confession the eyebrows narrowed and his lined face squinted up at the scribble.

DC Stubbs along with a forensic photographer had found the freezer and lifted the lid. It took a few seconds to comprehend. The tall young DC pulled back and heaved a couple of times while the photographer took pictures.

Although an initial hand writing comparison between the suicide note and the diary of Lydia Perkins confirmed it was the same person. A formal check by an expert would be required.

Within an hour, the crime scene had been taped off and the house was filled with a forensic team wearing white boiler suits and masks.

A police pathologist had called. He'd poked, prodded, photographed, taken samples and tagged what were the remains of three people.

Later, with labelled forensic plastic bags containing heads, feet and hands, the grisly contents were placed in a mortuary van and taken away.

By ten o'clock that evening their work was done for the day and all that remained was the perimeter tape and a police patrol car on guard through the night.

This chilled October evening the officers had the windows up as they tucked into their coffee and sandwiches. With the car radio on for music through the night they didn't hear the sounds coming from No 22 Roslin Gardens, Acton. The banging on the sink top. *'YES! YES! YES! OH GOD!'*